Guide to

Marine Mammals of Alaska

By Kate Wynne
Illustrated by Pieter Folkens

Sea Grant

MAB-44
Price: $20.00

Alaska Sea Grant College Program
University of Alaska Fairbanks
Fairbanks, AK 99775-5040
(907) 474-6707
Fax (907) 474-6285

Author Biography

Since 1981, Kate Wynne has been involved in assessing marine mammal populations and their interactions with commercial fisheries. Her studies include the survey, capture, and necropsy of more than twelve species of marine mammals in New England and Alaska, including cetaceans, pinnipeds, and sea otters. She has worked eight years as a marine mammal observer, has designed and coordinated marine mammal observer programs, and continues to train fishery observers in mammal identification. She earned her master's degree in wildlife management from the University of Maine, and currently is associate professor at the University of Alaska Fairbanks.

As marine mammal specialist for the Alaska Sea Grant Marine Advisory Program in Kodiak, one of Wynne's missions is to provide information for understanding and complying with complex and changing marine mammal laws. She believes that informed and cooperative resource users are vital to collecting reliable scientific data about marine resources—including mammals. Her research experience and her contact with fishermen, biologists, and observers inspired her to provide this book to help identify marine mammals in Alaska.

Acknowledgments

Enthusiastic support of this publication is testimony to the communal concern for and appreciation of the marine mammal resources of Alaska.

Funding was provided by the National Marine Fisheries Service, Office of Protected Resources, Silver Spring, MD; U.S. Fish and Wildlife Service, Marine Mammals Management, Anchorage, AK; Pacific States Marine Fisheries Commission, Portland, OR; and Marine Mammal Commission, Washington, DC.

Species account reviewers are: Marilyn Dahlheim, Tony DeGange, Rich Ferrero, Charles Fowler, Kathy Frost, Pat Gearin, Camille Goebel-Diaz, Harriet Huber, Brendan Kelly, Tom Loughlin, Dale Rice, David Rugh, Scott Schliebe, Dana Seagars, John Sease, Ward Testa, David Withrow, and Allen Wolman.

A special thanks to Carrie LeDuc, Kathy Frost, and Jon Nickles for reviewing the final drafts of this guide, and to Kurt Byers for his early inspiration and assistance seeking funding and photographs. And thanks to the many readers who sent comments and helped improve the second edition.

Table of Contents

Preface

Marine mammals have captured public interest as unique, intelligent, and sometimes competitive marine inhabitants. They have played an integral role in Native Alaskan culture for thousands of years, providing food, shelter, clothing, and handicrafts for coastal residents. In the United States, marine mammals have been federally protected since passage of the Marine Mammal Protection Act of 1972 and have gained popularity among marine recreationists and the general public. Drastic increases and decreases in some marine mammal populations have generated recent concern among marine resource users, biologists, and managers about the health of marine ecosystems and effects of human interactions with marine mammals. Arctic and coastal development pose increasing threats of disturbance, mortality, and oil contamination.

While marine mammal viewing and species identification remain a popular form of recreation, some federal species-specific regulations now require accurate identification of marine mammals. Commercial fishermen are required to identify marine mammals and report the species that interact with their gear. Federal marine resource observers are trained to identify marine mammals seen while monitoring commercial fishing operations. Even whale-watching vessels and tour boats now must follow federal guidelines when approaching whales.

This guide was inspired by the needs and desires of the diverse marine resource users who share Alaska's waters with marine mammals. It is designed to familiarize the observer with marine mammal characteristics and present species descriptions in a format that encourages fast, accurate identification at sea. It is intended to be informative yet readable, complete yet brief, and equally useful in a fisherman's wheelhouse, tour boat stateroom, or biologist's backpack. The book is printed on water resistant paper so that it will withstand hard wear and wet conditions.

The geographic scope of this guide has been limited to allow fast field identification of the nearly 30 Alaska species. We acknowledge the world distribution of each species but focus on their approximate distribution in waters surrounding Alaska: the North Pacific Ocean (including the Gulf of Alaska and Bering Sea) and the Arctic Ocean (including the Chukchi and Beaufort seas). A map of the area covered by this book is on the inside back cover.

Using This Book to Identify Marine Mammals

Accurate identification of marine mammals at sea often requires rapid incorporation of many clues during brief and distant visual contact. The physical traits, location (geographic and local habitat), and behavior of the animal are all important clues to note when viewing marine mammals and differentiating similar species. Tips:

1. Know what characteristics to look for. Review guides prior to your trip, and know what features are most helpful in species identification.

2. Be patient and persistent. Continue scanning the area—it may be several minutes before a marine mammal resurfaces.

3. Don't lose observation time thumbing through a field guide. Keep your eye on the mammal and make mental notes or quick sketches of key traits for later comparison with guides.

4. Don't jump to conclusions. Some marine mammal behavior is misleading. Pinnipeds and sea otters often break the surface (porpoise) while swimming fast, and several cetaceans sleep motionless at the surface. Continue observing to verify identification.

   Never base identification on behavior alone. Have at least two physical characteristics to make a positive identification.

5. This guide is specifically designed to aid accurate identification of mammals at sea.

   • Color-coded sections separate cetaceans and pinnipeds from other marine mammals.

   • Composite diagrams of species drawn to scale allow size and trait comparisons at a glance.

   • Gender identification and morphological traits are illustrated.

   • Species are grouped by family and presented in descending order by adult size.

   • Range maps show generalized seasonal distribution of each species: pink = summer, blue = winter, purple = year-round.

   • Key characteristics are presented in **bold** text.

   • Silhouette surface profiles accentuate traits visible at sea under poor light conditions.

   • Silhouette profiles are presented for direct comparison of species with similar traits and distribution.

   • Glossary on page 72 defines terms used in the text.

What Are Marine Mammals?

Mammals are animals that breathe air through lungs, are warm-blooded, have hair (at some time during life), bear young alive, and suckle their young.

Marine mammals are a diverse group thought to have evolved from terrestrial ancestors to aquatic life through a number of unique physical adaptations. Representatives are found in every ocean, on every continent, and in a variety of ecological roles, including herbivores (manatees), filter feeders (baleen whales), and apex predators (killer whales).

In this book we present three groups of Alaska marine mammals in order from most to least aquatic specialization: cetaceans (whales, dolphins, and porpoises), pinnipeds (seals, sea lions, and walrus), and marine fissipeds (sea otter and polar bear).

Cetaceans and pinnipeds exhibit extraordinary anatomical and physiological adaptations to a marine existence. Consider the physical demands on a warm-blooded, air-breathing animal living an amphibious or totally marine existence. Marine mammals have adapted to the extreme temperatures, depths, pressure, darkness, and density of the medium they live in.

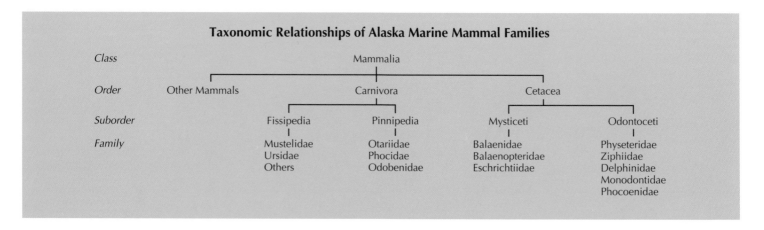

Taxonomic Relationships of Alaska Marine Mammal Families

Class		Mammalia		
Order	Other Mammals	Carnivora	Cetacea	
Suborder		Fissipedia / Pinnipedia	Mysticeti	Odontoceti
Family		Mustelidae / Ursidae / Others	Otariidae / Phocidae / Odobenidae	Balaenidae / Balaenopteridae / Eschrichtiidae	Physeteridae / Ziphiidae / Delphinidae / Monodontidae / Phocoenidae

Marine Adaptations

Deep Diving

Generally, marine mammal lungs are proportionately smaller than humans' but they:

- Use oxygen more efficiently. They fill their lungs and exchange 90% of their air in each breath, have high blood volume, and their blood chemistry allows greater oxygen retention (the high red blood cell count and increased myoglobin make their muscle tissue and blood dark red).

Kate Wynne

- Have a high tolerance to lactic acid and carbon dioxide. Their muscles can work anaerobically (without oxygen) while they hold their breath.
- Can tolerate tremendous atmospheric pressure at great depths. Lungs and ribs are collapsible, air spaces are minimized, and nitrogen absorption is limited.

Swimming Adaptations

- Drag is reduced by hydrodynamic body forms.
- Appendages are modified for maximal propulsion and minimal drag.

Thermoregulation

- A large body with small surface to volume ratio reduces heat loss. Blubber or thick underfur is used as insulation.

Marine mammals such as this harbor seal have streamlined bodies with modified appendages that increase their swimming
◄ **and thermal efficiency.**

- Complex circulatory system in extremities is used to conserve and dissipate heat.
- Young pinnipeds and cetaceans grow fast on milk with 40-50% fat (human milk is 3.3% fat).

Water Conservation

Most marine mammals rarely drink fresh water; instead they:

- Utilize water present in their food, inspired air, and blubber.
- Have specialized kidneys which produce urine that is saltier than sea water.

Sensory Adaptations

- Marine mammals communicate under water with sound, and many species use sound (echolocation) to locate prey. Tactile senses are acute. Pinnipeds and fissipeds have well-developed facial whiskers.

Cetaceans are completely aquatic mammals: they feed, mate, calve, and suckle their young in the water. They are the most specialized mammalian swimmers. Some are capable of maintaining speeds up to 25 mph, diving to depths to 10,000 ft, and remaining submerged up to 2 hrs. The body is streamlined (limbs are tapered or lacking) and the tail is developed into horizontal flukes for propulsion. The smooth, supple, and hairless skin further reduces drag during swimming.

Cetaceans breathe through nostrils (blowhole) on top of the head. When surfacing after a dive, whales forcefully expel the previous lungful of air (blow) and inspire new air. Characteristics of the blow are useful for identification.

Cetaceans are grouped into two taxonomic suborders: the baleen whales (Mysticeti) and the toothed whales (Odontoceti). Mysticetes are filterfeeders that forage for zooplankton and small fish by skimming or gulping huge amounts of prey and water. The water is then forced back out the mouth past hundreds of baleen plates that act as sieves to trap the prey, which is then swallowed.

Odontocetes have various numbers of identical conical or spade-shaped teeth that are used to strain or grasp prey, primarily fish and squid.

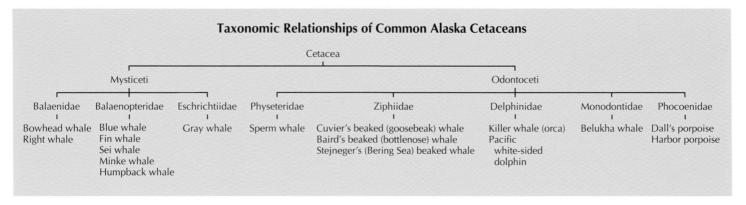

Taxonomic Relationships of Common Alaska Cetaceans

Cetacea

Mysticeti — Odontoceti

Balaenidae	Balaenopteridae	Eschrichtiidae	Physeteridae	Ziphiidae	Delphinidae	Monodontidae	Phocoenidae
Bowhead whale Right whale	Blue whale Fin whale Sei whale Minke whale Humpback whale	Gray whale	Sperm whale	Cuvier's beaked (goosebeak) whale Baird's beaked (bottlenose) whale Stejneger's (Bering Sea) beaked whale	Killer whale (orca) Pacific white-sided dolphin	Belukha whale	Dall's porpoise Harbor porpoise

Mysticetes (Baleen Whales)

All mysticetes have two nostrils. Females are generally larger than males but otherwise there is no sexual dimorphism. They are not known to echolocate prey. All three families are found in Alaska waters.

Balaenidae
(Right whales):
Robust body.
Skim prey using hundreds of long baleen plates. High arching lower lip and massive head (makes up a third of body length) are needed to accommodate baleen plates. No dorsal fin or ventral throat grooves. Nostrils separated into two divergent blowholes, creates V-shaped blow.

Balaenopteridae
(Rorquals): Numerous ventral throat grooves allow expansion for large-volume gulping of prey and water. Dorsal fin present. Single, straight blow.

Eschrichtiidae
(Gray whale):
Skim or dredge mud for crustaceans. Robust body with no dorsal fin or ventral throat grooves. Two to seven short, deep creases on throat. Baleen short and yellow.

Odontocetes (Toothed Whales)

All odontocetes have only one nostril leading to blowhole. Sexual dimorphism is common—males are larger than females, and diagnostic secondary sex traits are present in some families (differences in dorsal fins, tooth pattern). Echolocation for prey is common. Five families are found in Alaska.

Physeteridae
(Sperm whale):
Huge, squared head with underslung lower jaw. Blowhole located at end of left side of head, so blow angles forward and to side.

Ziphiidae
(Beaked whales): Various degrees of beak and dorsal fin development. Deep, long divers.

Delphinidae
(Dolphins):
Beak present. Prominent dorsal fin and melon. Conical teeth. Shallow divers.

Monodontidae
(Belukha):
No dorsal fin. Prominent melon.

Phocoenidae
(Porpoises):
No beak. Dorsal fin present. Spade-shaped teeth.

Note: Figures on this page show general body shapes. The whales are not drawn to scale.

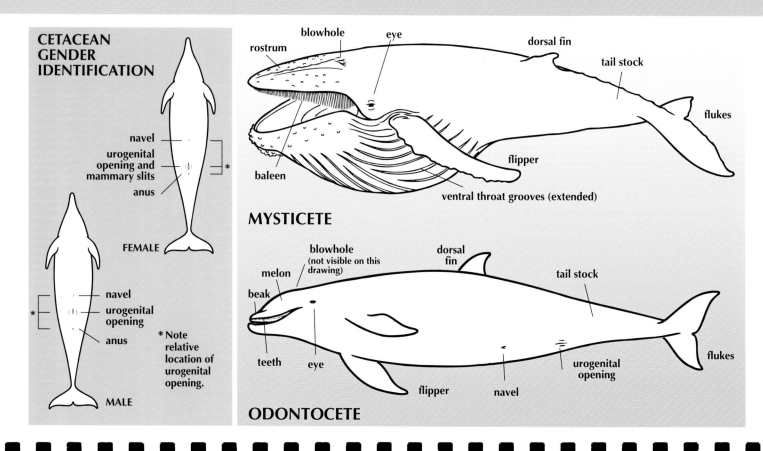

CETACEAN GENDER IDENTIFICATION

navel

urogenital opening and mammary slits

anus

*

FEMALE

navel

urogenital opening

anus

*

MALE

* Note relative location of urogenital opening.

rostrum

blowhole

eye

dorsal fin

tail stock

flukes

baleen

flipper

ventral throat grooves (extended)

MYSTICETE

blowhole (not visible on this drawing)

melon

dorsal fin

tail stock

beak

teeth

eye

flipper

navel

urogenital opening

flukes

ODONTOCETE

Minke Whale

Gray Whale

Humpback Whale

Dall's Porpoise

Pacific White-Sided Dolphin

Harbor Porpoise

Killer Whale

Sei Whale

Bowhead Whale

Fin Whale

Right Whale

Blue Whale

Stejneger's Beaked Whale

Belukha Whale

Sperm Whale

Baird's Beaked Whale

Cuvier's Beaked Whale

Common Cetaceans of Alaska

7

| 0 | 5 | 10 | 15 | FEET |
| 0 | 1 | 2 | 3 | 4 | 5 | METERS |

Bowhead Whale

Pieter Folkens

SIZE: Max 60 ft (18 m), max wt 75 tons. Length at birth 10-15 ft (3-4.5 m).

BODY: Robust body with **smooth skin** and massive head. High arching upper jaws hold up to 350 dark baleen plates per side, each to 12 ft (3.6 m) long. Bowed lower lips enfold a narrow rostrum. Flippers short and spatulate.

COLOR: Predominantly black with **white chin patch.** Some have white on tail stock.

DORSAL FIN: No dorsal fin. Back smooth.

BLOW: V-shaped, bushy, to 18 ft (5.5 m) high.

BEHAVIOR: Slow swimmers. Can break through 1-2 ft thick ice with head. Usually single or groups of ≤3 but aggregations of 50-60 may occur on feeding grounds. Highly vocal during migration.

DIVE PATTERN: Dive duration 15-20 min. Surface interval is 3-5 min.

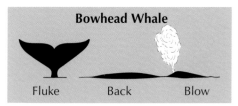

Bowhead Whale

Fluke   Back   Blow

CAN BE CONFUSED WITH:

Northern Right Whale

H. Braham

Note smooth, high-arched rostrum, v-shaped blow, and white lower lip.

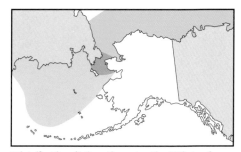

Distribution/Migration: Arctic. Winter in Bering Sea and follow leads in ice n. to summer feeding grounds in Chukchi and Beaufort seas. Often seen migrating n. with belukhas.

Michael Newcomer

HABITAT: Rarely far from ice.

FOOD HABITS: Zooplankton specialists. Prey on small to medium size copepods, euphausids, amphipods. Skim through large schools with mouth agape. May eat up to 3000 lbs per day.

LIFE HISTORY: Sexually mature at 12-20 yrs. Female has 1 calf every 3-7 yrs. Single calves born Apr-May after gestation of 12-16 mos. Lactation lasts about 1 yr.

STATUS AND HUMAN INTERACTIONS: Endangered but increasing. Approx 7500 in Bering Sea. Current harvest limited to subsistence use by AK Natives who are allowed to strike ≤54 or harvest ≤41 per yr. Noise from offshore oil activities has potential impact on migrating bowheads.

This view from top of harvested bowhead shows long, fringed baleen plates extending from rostrum. Eye is located in upper left of photo.

Bowhead Whale

Balaena mysticetus
Family: Balaenidae

Northern Right Whale

Pieter Folkens

SIZE: Max length 56 ft (17 m), avg wt 60 tons. Females larger than males. Length at birth 15-20 ft (4.6-6 m).

BODY: Robust body with large head (one fourth body length). Bowed lower lips enfold narrow, arching rostrum. **Callosities** (wart-like growths) on the rostrum, lower lip, and around the eyes. Up to 250 dark baleen plates per side, each to 9 ft (2.8 m) long. Flippers broad and spatulate.

COLOR: Predominantly black, some white patches on belly.

DORSAL FIN: No dorsal fin.

BLOW: V-shaped, bushy, to 16 ft (5 m) high.

BEHAVIOR: Docile. Slow swimmers but are more acrobatic than bowheads (often breaching, flipper slapping). Vocalization is variety of moans and burps.

DIVE PATTERN: Shallow divers. Blow once per 1-2 min. Max dive is 15 min.

Northern Right Whale

Fluke | Back | Blow

CAN BE CONFUSED WITH:

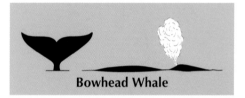

Bowhead Whale

Franz Kraus/New England Aquarium

Note the bonnet of callosities on high-arching rostrum and lower lip on the northern right whale.

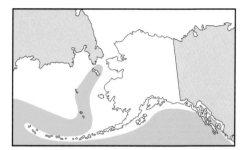

Distribution/Migration: N. Hemisphere. Migratory but population level so low in N. Pacific that patterns are unclear. Historically, s. Bering Sea and Gulf of AK were primary summer range. May winter as far s. as Baja California.

Note: All photo-documented right whale sightings in North Pacific waters are of great value to whale researchers !

HABITAT: Mostly temperate and subpolar waters. Calving may occur in shallow bays and coastal waters.

FOOD HABITS: Zooplankton specialists: primary prey is euphausids and copepods, gathered by skimming through schools with mouth agape.

LIFE HISTORY: Uncertain but probably breed in winter-spring at low latitudes and calve the following winter after gestation of 12 months. Single calf every 2-4 yrs. Lactation lasts 1 yr.

STATUS AND HUMAN INTERACTIONS: Endangered. Populations were decimated by commercial whalers who named it the right whale because it is easily approached, floats when killed, and is rich in oil. Completely protected since 1935 but population remains critically low (100-200). A sighting of 3-4 right whales with a calf in w. Bristol Bay in Jul 1996 was the first confirmation of reproduction in AK waters in decades.

Northern Right Whale

Eubalaena glacialis
Family: Balaenidae

Pieter Folkens

SIZE: Avg adult 85 ft (26 m), 100 tons. At birth 23 ft (7 m), 5500 lbs. Earth's largest animal ever.

BODY: Huge, sleek body. **Broad, flat, U-shaped rostrum** (when viewed from above) with up to 400 broad, black, 3 ft long (1m) baleen plates per side. Flippers long, slender, pointed. Flukes broad with notched, straight trailing edge. 55-68 ventral throat grooves.

COLOR: Body **blue-gray** with light **mottling.** Tongue, palate, and **baleen black.**

DORSAL FIN: Small (1 ft high), variable shape, **located far aft** (three-fourths head-tail distance), and often not seen until diving.

BLOW: Dense (not bushy), vertical blow to 30 ft (9 m) high.

BEHAVIOR: Travel alone or in pairs. Fast swimmers (bursts of up to 20 knots).

DIVE PATTERN: 1 blow every 1-2 min. Normal dive is 3-10 min, max is 20 min. **May raise flukes slightly.**

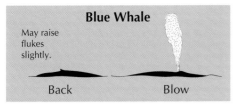

Blue Whale

May raise flukes slightly.

Back | Blow

CAN BE CONFUSED WITH:

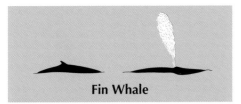

Fin Whale

Distribution/Migration: Worldwide. In N. Pacific, migrate to summer feeding grounds from CA n. into e. Gulf of AK, along Aleutians, and into Bering Sea. Migrate s. to wintering-calving grounds 1-10°N.

Sally Mizroch

▲
Tiny dorsal fin is far aft on huge, mottled, light blue back of the blue whale.

Gerry Joyce

HABITAT: Pelagic but may be seen near ice edge while migrating.

FOOD HABITS: Specialists. Eat primarily euphausids. May fast much of winter but consume estimated 4 tons per day during peak summer feeding periods.

LIFE HISTORY: Sexually mature at 10 yrs. Breed in fall and winter. Single calf every 2-3 yrs after gestation of 12 mos. Lactation lasts 7 mos. Calves gain 200 lbs per day (or 8 lbs per hr). May live 80 yrs.

STATUS AND HUMAN INTERACTIONS: Endangered, completely protected since 1965. Current population estimates: 12,000 worldwide, 1200-1700 in N. Pacific. Commercially overharvested: estimated 350,000 killed between 1860s and 1960s.

◄
Note broad flat rostrum, open nostrils, and mottled back of blue whale.

Blue Whale

Balaenoptera musculus
Family: Balaenopteridae

13

Kodiak Island 8/05

Pieter Folkens

SIZE: Avg adult male 70 ft (21 m), 45 tons. Avg adult female 73 ft (22 m), 45 tons. At birth 21 ft (6.5 m), 3600 lbs.

BODY: Large sleek body. Rostrum **V-shaped** and flat with up to 475 two ft long (0.7 m) gray or white baleen plates per side. 55-100 ventral throat grooves. **Distinct ridge** on back from dorsal fin to **broad triangular** flukes.

COLOR: Dark gray with light undersides, **pale chevron** on dorsal neck surface. Asymetrical jaw coloration: lower **right jaw white** but **left jaw dark.**

DORSAL FIN: Up to 2 ft tall, falcate with blunt tip and steep backward angle, located two-thirds distance between head and tail. **Appears shortly after blow.**

BLOW: Cone-like or elliptical, 18-20 ft (6 m) high.

BEHAVIOR: Often seen in groups of 6-10, alone or in pairs. Fast swimmers (bursts to 20 mph).

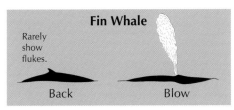

Fin Whale

Rarely show flukes.

Back   Blow

CAN BE CONFUSED WITH:

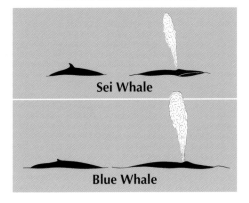

Sei Whale

Blue Whale

Note low angle of fin whale's blunt dorsal fin. ▶

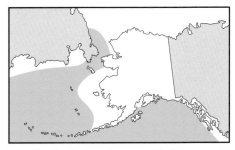

Distribution/Migration: Worldwide. In e. N. Pacific, winter from central CA s., migrate n. as far as Chukchi Sea to summer feeding grounds in Gulf of AK, Prince William Sound, along Aleutians.

P.R. Kelly

DIVE PATTERN: Rarely show flukes. Produce 4-5 blows at 10-20 sec intervals, then dive for 5-15 min. Max depth is 1000 ft (300 m).

HABITAT: Generally pelagic but may use deep coastal waters.

FOOD HABITS: Generalists. Prey on variety of small schooling fish and invertebrates by gulping large swarms while swimming on side. Feed primarily in summer. → krill

LIFE HISTORY: Sexually mature at 6-12 yrs. Breed in winter. Single calf every 2+ yrs born in winter after gestation of 11-12 mos. Lactation lasts 6 mos. May live 100 yrs.

STATUS AND HUMAN INTERACTIONS: Endangered. Population estimate: 75,000 worldwide. 16,000 in e. N. Pacific. Commercially harvested in N. Pacific until 1976.

Fin Whale

Balaenoptera physalus
Family: Balaenopteridae

Pieter Folkens

SIZE: Avg adult male 46 ft (14 m), 14 tons. Avg adult female 49 ft (15 m), 17 tons. At birth 15 ft (4.5 m), 1 ton.

BODY: Sleek dark body with pointed rostrum holding up to 400 2.7 ft long (0.8 m) dark baleen plates per side. Flippers slender and pointed. Large, notched flukes. 32-60 **short ventral throat grooves.**

COLOR: Uniformly dark gray with pale belly. Frequent light mottling and patches. **Both lower lips gray.**

DORSAL FIN: Fairly **erect, falcate,** about 2 ft high and located two-thirds distance between head and tail. **Often visible with blow.**

BLOW: Elliptical, to 10 ft (3 m) high. Similar in shape but shorter than fin whale's blow.

BEHAVIOR: Fastest swimming baleen whale (to 20 knots). Commonly seen alone or in groups of 2-5.

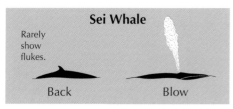

Sei Whale

Rarely show flukes.

Back Blow

CAN BE CONFUSED WITH:

Fin Whale

Note erect, strongly falcate dorsal fin on sei whale. ▸

Distribution/Migration: Worldwide. Migrate between high-latitude summer feeding grounds and low-latitude winter breeding grounds. In e. N. Pacific, spend summers from CA to Gulf of AK and winters from central CA south, possibly to equator.

Michael Newcomer

DIVE PATTERN: 2-3 blows at 20 sec intervals between dives lasting 5-6 min. 5-6 blows between dives lasting 15-30 min. Shallow divers, **seldom show flukes when diving.**

HABITAT: Pelagic.

FOOD HABITS: Generalists. Skim through schools of crustaceans (mainly copepods but also amphipods, euphausids), small fish, and squid. May eat 1 ton per day.

LIFE HISTORY: Sexually mature at 10 yrs. Breed mostly in winter. Single calf every 3 yrs after gestation of 11.5-12 mos. Lactation lasts 6-9 mos. May live 60 yrs.

STATUS AND HUMAN INTERACTIONS: Endangered. In N. Pacific population is protected and estimated at 14,000. Commercially harvested worldwide until 1977.

Sei Whale

Balaenoptera borealis
Family: Balaenopteridae

17

Pieter Folkens

SIZE: Avg adult male 26 ft (8 m), 6 tons. Avg adult female 28 ft (8.5 m), 8 tons. At birth 10 ft (3 m), 1000 lbs.

BODY: Small and sleek. **Head is sharply pointed** with flat rostrum. Up to 285 eight in. long (0.2 m) baleen plates per side ranging from dark gray to yellow. Flippers pointed. Broad flukes. 50-70 ventral throat grooves. Smallest baleen whale in the N. Pacific.

COLOR: Black or dark steel gray. Lighter undersides, often with a pale chevron on back behind head. **White patch on both flippers.**

DORSAL FIN: Prominent and falcate, located two-thirds distance between head and tail. **Appears simultaneously with blow.**

BLOW: Low, bushy, and inconspicuous.

BEHAVIOR: Fast swimmers, often approach boats. Solitary or in groups of 2-3. May breach.

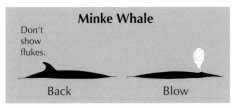

Minke Whale

Don't show flukes.

Back   Blow

CAN BE CONFUSED WITH:

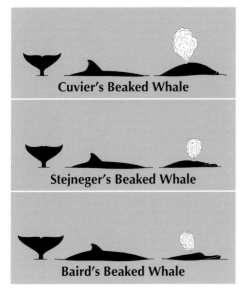

Cuvier's Beaked Whale

Stejneger's Beaked Whale

Baird's Beaked Whale

Distribution/Migration: Worldwide. In N. Pacific, found throughout ice-free AK waters in summer. Most spend winters in subtropics (20-25°N).

Brent Stewart

◄ Note pointed rostrum and prominent white patch on flipper of minke whale.

DIVE PATTERN: 5-8 blows at <1 min intervals between dives up to 20 min long. Arch tail stock high but **don't show flukes.**

HABITAT: Both pelagic and common in bays and shallow coastal waters, often in and near ice.

FOOD HABITS: Feed primarily in summer. Prey on variety of schooling fish and zooplankton.

LIFE HISTORY: Sexually mature at 6 yrs. May breed throughout the year. Single calf every 1-2 yrs after gestation of 10-11 mos. Lactation is 6 mos. May live >50 yrs.

STATUS AND HUMAN INTERACTIONS: Status unknown; perhaps 9000 in N. Pacific. Still commercially harvested in S. Hemisphere.

Minke Whale

Balaenoptera acutorostrata
Family: Balaenopteridae

19

Kodiak Island 8/05

Pieter Folkens

SIZE: Avg adult male 46 ft (14 m), 25 tons. Avg adult female 49 ft (15 m), 35 tons. At birth 16 ft (5 m), 2 tons.

BODY: Stocky body with flat, broad head. **Series of fleshy knobs on rostrum and lower lip.** Up to 400 two ft long (0.7 m) dark baleen plates per side and 12-36 ventral throat grooves. **Flippers elongate** (one-third body length) and **flukes broad** with irregular trailing edge.

COLOR: Body black with some white on throat and belly. **White on flippers and flukes.**

DORSAL FIN: Fin small, shape varies (can distinguish individuals). Seen at same time as blow.

BLOW: Broad and bushy, to 10 ft (3 m) high.

BEHAVIOR: Usually congregate in groups of 2-12 but larger congregations are common on both winter and summer grounds. **Acrobatic:** breaching, spyhopping, and lobtailing are common.

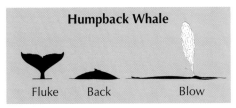

Humpback Whale

Fluke   Back   Blow

CAN BE CONFUSED WITH:

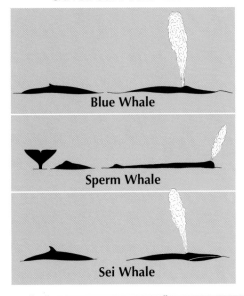

Blue Whale

Sperm Whale

Sei Whale

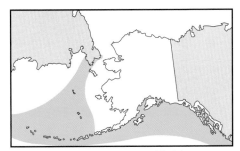

Distribution/Migration: Worldwide. In N. Pacific, migrate from winter breeding grounds in Hawaiian and Mexican waters to summer feeding grounds from WA to Chukchi Sea.

Jan Straley Sitka, AK

Variety of vocalizations including complex songs.

DIVE PATTERN: Blow 4-10 times at 20-30 sec intervals between dives lasting 3-28 mins. **Flukes show prior to deep dives.**

HABITAT: Pelagic and coastal. Feed and breed over shallow banks but may traverse open ocean during migration.

FOOD HABITS: Prey on euphausids and small schooling fish; some use bubbles to help capture prey.

LIFE HISTORY: Sexually mature at 4-7 yrs. Breed in winter. Single calf born every 1-3 yrs after gestation of 11.5 mos. Lactation lasts 6-10 mos. May live 50 yrs.

STATUS AND HUMAN INTERACTIONS: Endangered. Approx 10,000 worldwide, <2000 in N. Pacific. Protected from commercial harvest since 1966.

Scalloped trailing edge and white undersides on fluke show before deep dives. Biologists use black and white patterns to recognize individual humpbacks.

Humpback Whale

Megaptera novaeangliae
Family: Balaenopteridae

Pieter Folkens

SIZE: Avg adult 46 ft (14 m), 33 tons. At birth 15 ft (4.5 m), 1100 lbs.

BODY: Body robust. Head profile triangular, upper jaw relatively narrow and arched with up to 180 (to 7 in. long, or 0.2 m) yellow baleen plates per side. **Patches of skin encrusted with barnacles.** 2-7 short throat creases. Flippers paddle-like and pointed. Flukes broad.

COLOR: Mottled gray, some orange patches caused by parasitic whale lice.

DORSAL FIN: No dorsal fin, but a **low hump** followed by several knobs on dorsal ridge of tail stock.

BLOW: Heart-shaped, to 10 ft (3 m) high.

BEHAVIOR: Group size usually 2-3. Breaching and lobtailing common. May approach boats on calving grounds.

DIVE PATTERN: Blow 4-6 times per min between dives of 3-5 min. **Usually raise flukes before a prolonged dive.**

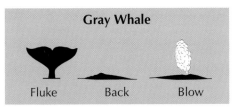

Gray Whale

Fluke	Back	Blow

CAN BE CONFUSED WITH:

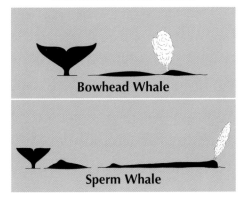

Bowhead Whale

Sperm Whale

Note gray, barnacle-encrusted body of the gray whale. Blow is heart-shaped when viewed from back or front. ▶

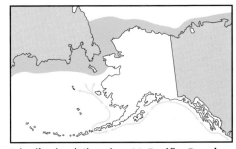

Distribution/Migration: N. Pacific. Breed and winter in Mexico and migrate n. through coastal waters (passing through Unimak Pass) to summer feeding grounds in the Bering, Chukchi, and Beaufort seas. Return s. in fall.

Pat Gearin NMML

HABITAT: Coastal, shallow waters over continental shelf.

FOOD HABITS: Only benthic-feeding whale: dredge through mud and use baleen to filter out bottom-dwelling amphipods and crustaceans. Often seen surfacing with mud streaming from mouth. Rarely feed in wintering grounds.

LIFE HISTORY: Sexually mature at 8 yrs. Breed in Nov-Dec during s. migration. Single calf every 2 yrs born Jan-Feb in and near lagoons in Baja California after gestation of 13.5 mos. Lactation lasts 7-9 mos.

STATUS AND HUMAN INTERACTIONS: Removed from Endangered Species List after numbers increased to a record high of approx 21,000 in the e. Pacific. Commercially harvested until 1947. Current annual harvest of 180-200 for Native Alaskan and Siberian subsistence. Heavy whale-watching and tourist traffic on migration and calving grounds.

Gray Whale

Eschrichtius robustus
Family: Eschrichtiidae

Pieter Folkens

SIZE: Avg adult male 50 ft (15 m), 40 tons. Avg adult female 36 ft (11 m), 22 tons. At birth 13 ft (4 m), 1 ton.

BODY: Huge, squared head (one-third body length). Approx 50 conical teeth, most growing from narrow, underslung lower jaw. **Body** (except for head) **appears wrinkled.**

COLOR: Dark gray, some lighter blotches on belly.

DORSAL FIN: Single smooth dorsal hump followed by series of "knuckles."

BLOW: Off-center, single blowhole. **Blow** is directed **forward at 45° angle and to the left.**

BEHAVIOR: Females and young form close social groups of 10-80 animals. Mature males form bachelor herds, whereas oldest males are often solitary. Often encountered resting at surface. Many reported mass strandings.

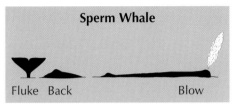

Sperm Whale

Fluke Back Blow

CAN BE CONFUSED WITH:

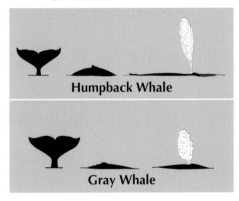

Humpback Whale

Gray Whale

Note sperm whale's square head, blow at 45° angle, wrinkled body, and low round dorsal fin. ▷

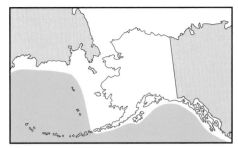

Distribution/Migration: Worldwide. Both sexes migrate toward equator in fall. Females, calves, and young males remain in tropical or temperate waters while older males migrate to higher latitudes in summer. Males occur as far n. as Bering Sea.

Gerry Joyce

DIVE PATTERN: Deepest and longest diving cetacean (dive for up to 90 min, possibly to 10,000 ft, or 3048 m). Swim slowly at surface for 15-60 minutes blowing at regular intervals. **Flukes usually show when diving.**

HABITAT: Pelagic, rarely seen in waters less than 650 ft deep (200 m).

FOOD HABITS: Squid specialists. Giant squid are preferred but also eat smaller squid and fish. May eat 1 ton of squid per day.

LIFE HISTORY: Sexually mature at 10 yrs. Old males join female schools during mating season. Single calf born every 3-15 yrs after 14-16 mos gestation. Lactation lasts 12-24 mos.

STATUS AND HUMAN INTERACTIONS: Endangered. Estimated 1.5 million worldwide, 930,000 in N. Pacific. Commercially harvested for oil until 1987.

Sperm Whale

Physeter macrocephalus
Family: Physeteridae

Belukha Whale

Kate Wynne

SIZE: Avg adult male 13 ft (4 m), 3300 lbs. Avg adult female 12 ft (3.7 m), 3000 lbs. At birth 5 ft (1.5 m), 100 lbs.

BODY: Stocky body with flexible neck. Small, rounded head with **prominent melon** and **short beak.** 40-44 conical teeth. Flippers broad and spatulate, edges curl with age. Flukes broad, notched, with convex trailing edges.

COLOR: Dark gray at birth, fade with age (blue-gray as juveniles) to **completely white** as adults (5-6 yrs).

DORSAL FIN: No dorsal fin. Narrow dorsal ridge along back, accentuated in older males.

BLOW: Low and inconspicuous, often heard rather than seen.

BEHAVIOR: Gregarious. Groups of 15-1000+ are common. Often associated with ice. Vocal but seldom acrobatic.

DIVE PATTERN: Slow swimmers, often roll casually at surface.

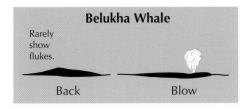

Belukha Whale

Rarely show flukes.

Back

Blow

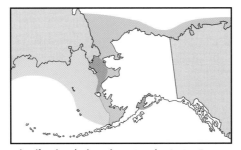

Distribution/Migration: Arctic. In N. Pacific, found seasonally in Cook Inlet, Bering, Chukchi, and Beaufort seas, often in or near ice. In summer, congregate in coastal and river systems.

Kathy Frost

HABITAT: Coastal or near ice.

FOOD HABITS: Generalists. 100+ known prey species include fish, squid, crabs, and clams. Echolocate prey with sophisticated sonar.

LIFE HISTORY: Sexually mature at 5-8 yrs. Breed in spring. Single calf every 2+ yrs after gestation of 14 mos. Lactation lasts 1-2 yrs. May live 35 years or more.

STATUS AND HUMAN INTERACTIONS: Stable; estimated 57,000 in AK waters. AK Natives harvest 200-400 annually for subsistence use. Coastal and river development, pollution, and net fisheries pose potential threats.

Belukhas are gregarious and often travel in large pods.

Kate Wynne

Note residual blue-gray pigment on subadult belukha.

Belukha Whale

Pieter Folkens

SIZE: Avg adult male 34 ft (10.4 m), 10 tons. Avg adult female 37 ft (11.3 m), 12.5 tons.

BODY: Robust, cylindrical body with relatively small, rounded flippers. **Well-defined, long, bottle-nose beak** and **prominent melon. Two** pairs of teeth at tip of lower jaw in both sexes. **Two** long, V-shaped throat grooves.

COLOR: Uniform slate gray with white patches on belly. **Scarring common.**

DORSAL FIN: Small, triangular, far aft.

BLOW: Low and wide.

BEHAVIOR: Generally shy and elusive around vessels. Occasionally found basking on the surface. Usually travel in pods of 2-20.

DIVE PATTERN: Surface three or four times at 20 sec intervals prior to deep dives lasting 20 min or more. Tight pods may surface synchronously. **Beak often visible when animal is surfacing.** May raise flukes when diving.

Baird's Beaked Whale

| Fluke | Back | Blow |

CAN BE CONFUSED WITH:

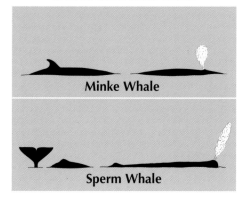

Minke Whale

Sperm Whale

Distribution/Migration: N. Pacific only. Unusual migration pattern. Move s. as far as CA in summer and range as far n. as St. Matthew Is. and the Pribilofs in winter.

HABITAT: Pelagic, generally in waters deeper than 3300 ft.

FOOD HABITS: Feed primarily on squid but also other deep-water species.

LIFE HISTORY: Sexually mature at 8-10 years. Mating occurs in autumn. Single calf every 2-3 yrs born in spring after gestation of 17 mos. May live 70 yrs.

STATUS AND HUMAN INTERACTIONS: Status unknown. Modest historic commercial harvest, currently 10-40 killed annually by Japanese whalers.

Michael Newcomer

Note triangular dorsal fins far aft on backs of tightly grouped Baird's whales.

Michael Newcomer

Note low, wide blow. Beaks and melons are visible when animals surface.

Baird's Beaked (Bottlenose) Whale

Berardius bairdii
Family: Ziphiidae

Pieter Folkens

SIZE: Avg adult male 20 ft (6 m), 4 tons. Avg adult female 21 ft (6.4 m), 5 tons.

BODY: Robust body. Sloping forehead and short beak. Flippers small and slightly tapered. Tiny median notch between flukes. **One pair of teeth at lower jaw** (do not erupt through gumline in females). One pair of V-shaped throat grooves.

COLOR: Body tan to reddish-brown. **Head and neck white in adults. Scarring common.**

DORSAL FIN: Relatively small, curved, far aft.

BLOW: Inconspicuous and low.

BEHAVIOR: Not frequently seen. Apparently avoid vessels. Travel in pods of 2-15. May breach.

DIVE PATTERN: Deep and long divers. Often a series of shallow surface dives at 20 sec intervals precedes 30 min deep dives. **Forehead breaks surface but beak**

Cuvier's Beaked Whale

Fluke   Back   Blow

CAN BE CONFUSED WITH:

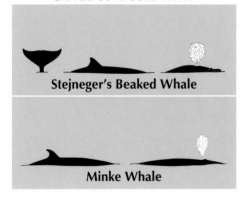

Stejneger's Beaked Whale

Minke Whale

Single pair of conical teeth erupt from forward tip of lower jaw of male Cuvier's beaked whale. ▶

Distribution: Worldwide. In N. Pacific, range north into Gulf of AK and the Aleutians.

Kate Wynne

not usually visible. Show flukes prior to deep dives.

HABITAT: Pelagic. Tropical and temperate waters deeper than 3300 ft.

FOOD HABITS: Poorly known. Thought to eat primarily squid. Deep-water fish as well as benthic invertebrates sometimes taken.

LIFE HISTORY: Poorly known. No marked breeding season. Single calves probably born year-round after unknown gestation period. Solitary strandings are fairly frequent.

STATUS AND HUMAN INTERACTIONS: Status unknown but assumed stable. Unknown number taken incidental to commercial fisheries worldwide. Potential dietary overlap with commercial squid fisheries.

Cuvier's Beaked (Goosebeak) Whale

Ziphius cavirostris
Family: Ziphiidae

31

Pieter Folkens

SIZE: Avg adult 16 ft (5 m), 1.3 tons.

BODY: Cylindrical body with small flippers. **Beak long,** well defined. **Lower lips arched near corner of mouth** (most predominantly in males). **One pair teeth large, flattened, triangular** located far back on lower jaw. **Protrude above the gumline in adult males.** One pair throat grooves.

COLOR: Few seen alive. Thought to be gray-brown on the back with lighter belly. Oval and linear scarring common.

DORSAL FIN: Small, curved, far aft.

BLOW: Low and inconspicuous.

BEHAVIOR: Form cohesive groups of 2-15 animals. Often travel abreast and may dive and surface in unison.

DIVE PATTERN: Several shallow, casual dives followed by longer dive of 10-15 min.

Stejneger's Beaked Whale

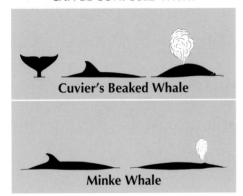

Fluke   Back   Blow

CAN BE CONFUSED WITH:

Cuvier's Beaked Whale

Minke Whale

Note scarred body, and pair of large triangular teeth at corner of mouth in male Stejneger's beaked whale. ▶

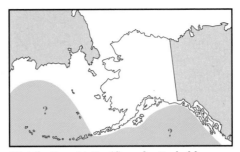

Distribution: N. Pacific only. Probably range from the Pribilofs and Bristol Bay south to Monterey, CA. Known only from strandings, which are most common in the Aleutians and coastal AK.

Kate Wynne

FOOD HABITS: Eat primarily squid but also fish.

HABITAT/LIFE HISTORY/STATUS: Unknown.

Kate Wynne

Skull of whale at left shows inward angle of flattened teeth. Leading edge of both teeth are worn with age.

Stejneger's (Bering Sea) Beaked Whale

Mesoplodon stejnegeri
Family: Ziphiidae

33

Pieter Folkens

SIZE: Avg adult male 26 ft (8 m), 8 tons. Avg adult female 23 ft (7 m), 4 tons. At birth 8 ft (2.4 m), 400 lbs.

BODY: Robust body. Round head with slight beak. Large paddle-like flippers.

COLOR: Striking contrast, black body with white chin, belly, and patch behind eye. Gray "saddle" behind dorsal fin.

DORSAL FIN: Prominent, up to 6 ft tall (2 m) on males, located midway on back. Sexually dimorphic (falcate on females, straight and much taller on males).

BLOW: Bushy, to 10 ft (3 m) high.

BEHAVIOR: Highly social, often travel in pods of 3-40. Acrobatic: breaching, spy-hopping, and lobtailing are common. Often cooperate in hunting and feeding efforts.

DIVE PATTERN: Variable. Many blows at short intervals between dives of 4-10 min.

HABITAT: Coastal waters to 500+ miles offshore.

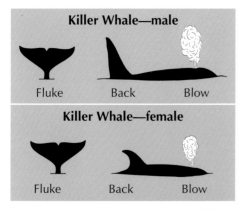

Killer Whale—male

Fluke · Back · Blow

Killer Whale—female

Fluke · Back · Blow

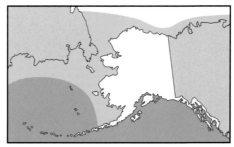

Distribution/Migration: Worldwide. In N. Pacific, transients and year-round residents found in ice-free waters of Gulf of AK, Aleutians, Bering, and Chukchi seas.

Kate Wynne

FOOD HABITS: Most diverse cetacean diet; includes fish, birds, squid, turtles, and marine mammals. Diets of two recognized killer whale stocks differ: "residents" eat primarily fish, while "transients" eat primarily marine mammals.

LIFE HISTORY: Sexually mature at 10-15 yrs. Mating and birth occur year-round. Single calf every 2+ yrs after gestation of 13-16 mos. Lactation lasts 12+ mos. May live >50 yrs.

STATUS AND HUMAN INTERACTIONS: Population probably stable. Live-captured for public display in U.S. and Canadian waters until 1977. Compete with some commercial fisheries. As apex predators, accumulate contaminants present in food chain.

Note identical, conical teeth, white eye patch, and short beak of killer whale.

Fred Felleman

Note paddle-like flippers and white pattern on belly of breaching orca.

Killer Whale (Orca)

Orcinus orca
Family: Delphinidae

35

Pacific White-Sided Dolphin

Michael Newcomer

SIZE: Avg adult length 7.5 ft (2.3 m), 300 lbs. At birth 3 ft (0.9 m).

BODY: Robust body with **short beak.**

COLOR: Black back and beak with white stripe ("suspenders") from forehead, along ribs to anus. **Light gray** from forehead **along sides.** Belly white.

DORSAL FIN: Tall, strongly **falcate,** with **two-tone** color. Forward third dark, trailing two-thirds light.

BLOW: Inconspicuous.

BEHAVIOR: Gregarious, often travel in multi-species herds of tens to several thousand animals. Acrobatic and common bowriders. Fast swimmers.

HABITAT: Mostly pelagic but also occur on continental shelf.

FOOD HABITS: Eat a variety of small schooling fish and squid.

Pacific White-Sided Dolphin

Breach

CAN BE CONFUSED WITH:

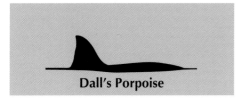

Dall's Porpoise

Distribution/Migration: N. Pacific only. Seasonal movements into temperate waters. Summer as far n. as Kodiak Is. Present in Aleutians and Gulf of AK.

LIFE HISTORY: Little known about reproductive history. May breed and calve spring-summer. Single calf born after 10-12 mo gestation. May live 45 yrs.

STATUS AND HUMAN INTERACTIONS: Common; estimated 480,000-931,000 in N. Pacific. Low level of commercial harvest by Japanese. Incidentally caught in offshore fisheries. Common oceanarium performers.

Kate Wynne

Naturally acrobatic, Pacific white-sided dolphins are easily trained as oceanarium performers.

Gerry Joyce

Compare splash pattern and location of white patches on Dall's porpoise (R) and Pacific white-sided dolphin (L), often seen traveling together.

Pacific White-Sided Dolphin

Lagenorhynchus obliquidens
Family: Delphinidae

Michael Newcomer

SIZE: Avg adult 6.4 ft (2 m), 300 lbs. At birth: approx 3 ft (1 m).

BODY: Stocky body with small flippers and flukes. **Small head, no distinct beak. Thick tail stock,** some with **prominent keel.** Teeth spade-like.

COLOR: Striking contrast: black body with white belly and flanks. Often **white on** trailing edge of **dorsal fin and flukes.**

DORSAL FIN: Triangular. Variable amount of white on trailing edge or upper half of dorsal fin.

BLOW: Inconspicuous.

BEHAVIOR: Fast, vigorous swimmers. Create **rooster-tail** of spray at high speeds or may roll slowly at surface. Common **bowriders.** Rarely acrobatic or clearing water's surface. May travel alone or in groups of 2-20.

DIVE PATTERN: Surface frequently and dive for 2-4 min. Dive depths unknown.

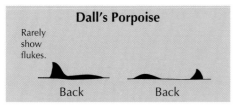

Dall's Porpoise

Rarely show flukes.

Back   Back

CAN BE CONFUSED WITH:

Harbor Porpoise

Pacific White-Sided Dolphin

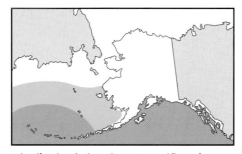

Distribution/Migration: N. Pacific only. Common from the Bering Sea and Gulf of AK (spring-summer) to coastal waters as far s. as Baja California (fall-winter). Present year-round in much of its ice-free range.

Kathy Frost

White side is visible beneath rooster-tail spray on fast-swimming Dall's porpoise. ▶

HABITAT: Pelagic and coastal in cool temperate to cold waters.

FOOD HABITS: Eat squid and a variety of fish.

LIFE HISTORY: Sexually mature at 3-4 yrs. Little known of breeding behavior. Single calf every yr after gestation of 11-12 mos. Lactation lasts 2-4 mos. May live 20 yrs.

STATUS AND HUMAN INTERACTIONS: Seasonally common in some regions. Previous high numbers of directed and incidental kills by Japanese have been reduced significantly. Currently, few are taken in coastal net fisheries off N. America and in high seas squid driftnet fisheries.

Dall's Porpoise

Phocoenoides dalli
Family: Phocoenidae

Harbor Porpoise

Kate Wynne

SIZE: Avg adult 5 ft (1.5 m), 120 lbs. At birth approx 30 in. (0.8 m).

BODY: Smallest AK cetacean. Stocky with small pointed flippers. **No beak.** Teeth spade-like.

COLOR: Dark gray or black on back with lighter sides and white belly.

DORSAL FIN: Small and **triangular.**

BLOW: Not often seen but may be heard under quiet conditions.

BEHAVIOR: Shy. May approach stationary vessels but generally avoid moving vessels and usually **do not bowride.** Not acrobatic. Generally travel alone or in groups of 2-10.

DIVE PATTERN: Shallow and frequent divers.

HABITAT: Cold coastal waters, usually in waters less than 300 ft deep.

FOOD HABITS: Eat schooling fish and invertebrates, including herring, mackerel, smelt, squid.

Harbor Porpoise

Don't show flukes.

Back

CAN BE CONFUSED WITH:

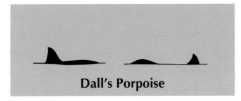

Dall's Porpoise

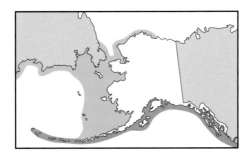

Kate Wynne

Distribution/Migration: N. Hemisphere. N. into Beaufort Sea in ice-free months, s. to s. California. May have seasonal movement patterns, but no known mass migration.

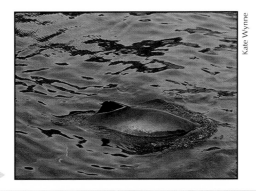

The harbor porpoise body is small with low, triangular dorsal fin. ▶

LIFE HISTORY: Sexually mature at 3-5 yrs. Breed in summer. Single calf every 1+ yrs after gestation of 10-11 mos. Lactation lasts approx 8 mos. May live 13 yrs.

STATUS AND HUMAN INTERACTIONS: Locally common, estimated 23,800-29,800 in AK. Incidentally killed in several coastal fisheries worldwide. Limited harvest for subsistence.

James R. Gilbert

Harbor porpoise are accidentally tangled in several gillnet fisheries. Those caught in surface nets may survive if released promptly and carefully.

Harbor Porpoise

Phocoena phocoena
Family: Phocoenidae

41

Pinnipeds are carnivores that have adapted to an amphibious marine existence. They forage at sea but most come ashore or onto ice at some time of the year to mate, give birth, suckle their young, or to molt. Many of their anatomical features reflect compromises needed to succeed in both marine and terrestrial environments. Externally, pinnipeds share many characteristics with terrestrial carnivores (fissipeds) due to their need for mobility on land.

Pinnipeds have four webbed flippers used to propel their spindle-shaped bodies. Their sensory organs are adapted to function both in air and water: large eyes and well-developed whiskers allow feeding in dimly lit water; tail and external ears are small, limiting drag. Pinnipeds have retained canine teeth but molars are modified for consuming prey whole. All have fur, which is shed or molted annually, but are insulated primarily by blubber. Pinnipeds

are present in habitats ranging from ice to tropics, coastal to pelagic waters, and may live a migratory or sedentary existence. They are opportunistic feeders and consume their varied prey whole or in chunks. Many pinnipeds are capable of long, deep repetitive dives (to 4500 ft depths and 2 hours). This phenomenal diving ability is possible because of several physiological traits shared by cetaceans, such as high blood volume and reduced heart rate.

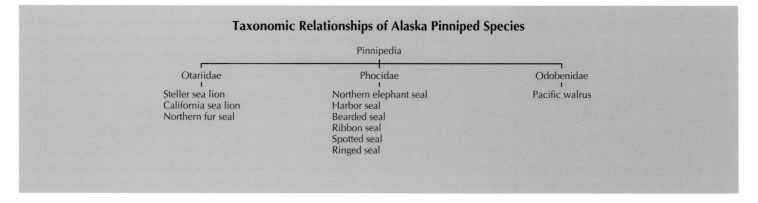

Taxonomic Relationships of Alaska Pinniped Species

Pinnipedia

Otariidae	Phocidae	Odobenidae
Steller sea lion	Northern elephant seal	Pacific walrus
California sea lion	Harbor seal	
Northern fur seal	Bearded seal	
	Ribbon seal	
	Spotted seal	
	Ringed seal	

Representatives of all three pinniped families are present in Alaska waters.

Otariidae ("eared" seals):

Otariids have visible external ear flaps (pinnae) and an elongate neck. They swim using their long front flippers for propulsion and hind flippers for steering. On land, otariids are agile and quadrupedal: able to pull their hind flippers up under the body and extend the front flippers for four-legged movement.

Adult otariids are sexually dimorphic: males are nearly twice as large as females, and have thickened necks and pronounced skull crests. Females breed with dominant males that establish and defend territories on breeding beaches or rookeries. Pups are born on the rookeries, suckling for the first 3-5 months. They may be dependent on their mothers for a year or more.

Phocidae ("earless" seals):

Phocids have no visible external ear flaps (pinnae). They have short necks and short front flippers, and cannot pull their hind flippers under the body while on land. Although graceful swimmers, phocids are not agile on land and typically move by undulating or heaving the body in a caterpillar-like manner.

Sexual dimorphism is rare in adult phocids (seen only in elephant seals); males and females are generally similar in size and shape. Phocids breed in the water, on shore, or on ice, but (except for elephant seals) don't breed on rookeries. Pups grow at an incredibly fast rate and are weaned young and abruptly after brief lactation during which their mothers probably fast.

Odobenidae (walrus):

The walrus body form combines phocid and otariid traits. They have no external ear flaps (pinnae) but move quadrupedally on land. The upper canines in both sexes elongate and develop into tusks.

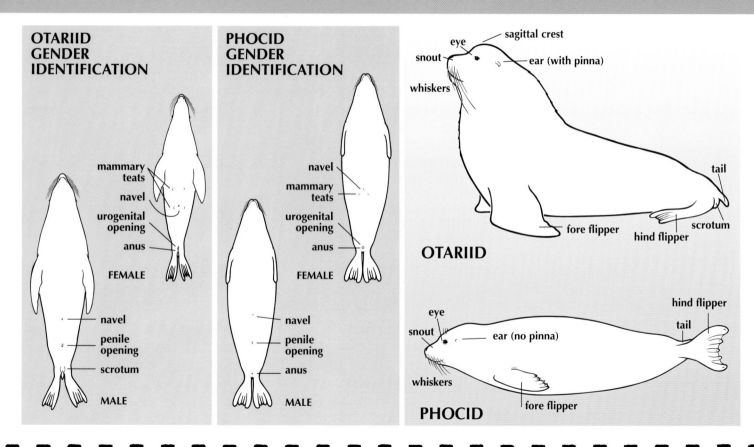

OTARIID
GENDER
IDENTIFICATION

mammary teats
navel
urogenital opening
anus

FEMALE

navel
penile opening
scrotum

MALE

PHOCID
GENDER
IDENTIFICATION

navel
mammary teats
urogenital opening
anus

FEMALE

navel
penile opening
anus

MALE

eye
sagittal crest
snout
ear (with pinna)
whiskers
tail
fore flipper
hind flipper
scrotum

OTARIID

eye
hind flipper
snout
tail
ear (no pinna)
whiskers
fore flipper

PHOCID

Harbor Seal

Ribbon Seal

Ringed Seal

Steller Sea Lion

♂

♀

Northern Fur Seal

♂

♀

California Sea Lion

♂

♀

Spotted Seal

Bearded Seal

Pacific Walrus

♂

♀

Northern Elephant Seal

♂

♀

Common Pinnipeds of Alaska

| 0 | 1 | 2 | 3 | FEET |
| 0 | | .5 | 1 | METER |

45

Harry Walker

SIZE: Avg adult male 9 ft (2.7 m), 1500 lbs. Avg adult female 7 ft (2.1 m), 600 lbs. At birth 3 ft (1 m), 45 lbs.

BODY: Robust body; males develop a thickened neck and mane with age. Large, bulging eyes, squared snout, and **obvious pinnae.**

COLOR: Dark brown at birth. Adult body **light brown to blond** with dark brown undersides and flippers. Appear **tan** in water.

BEHAVIOR: Gregarious. Gather on haulouts and rookeries. Generally aggressive. Vocalizations are grumbles, growls, and roars but they **do not bark.** Dive capabilities unknown but may dive to 600 ft (180 m).

HABITAT: Primarily coastal. Use secluded rocky islands for haulouts and rookeries.

FOOD HABITS: Opportunistic. Eat fish, squid, and shrimp. Males fast while holding territories.

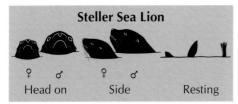

Steller Sea Lion

♀ Head on ♂   ♀ Side ♂   Resting

CAN BE CONFUSED WITH:

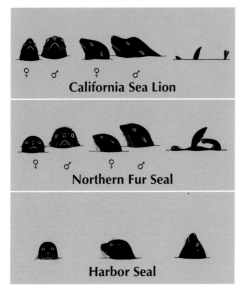

♀ ♂   ♀ ♂
California Sea Lion

♀ ♂   ♀
Northern Fur Seal

Harbor Seal

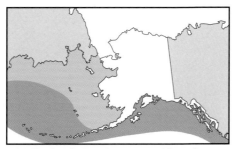

Distribution/Migration: N. Pacific only. In e. N. Pacific, range from s. CA n. through Gulf of AK, Bering Sea, and Aleutians. Seasonal movements common, migration unknown.

Harriet Huber

LIFE HISTORY: Sexually mature at 3-7 yrs. Females breed with dominant males that establish and defend territories up to 60 days. Single pup per yr born in May-Jul after gestation of 11.5 mos. Lactation lasts 1-3 yrs. Female leaves 1-3 mo-old pup on shore during extended foraging bouts. Females may live 30 yrs. Molting takes place Jul-Nov.

STATUS AND HUMAN INTERACTIONS: Estimated 100,000-140,000 worldwide, approx 58,000 in AK. Endangered and declining w. of 144°W longitude; Threatened and stable eastward. AK Natives harvest <500/yr for meat and fur. Frequent take by commercial fishermen in 1970s and 1980s has been reduced and is monitored by federal observers. Competition with several commercial fisheries in Bering Sea and Gulf of AK may exist but is poorly documented.

Note the differences in profile and color of Steller (light) and California sea lion (dark) in water.

Steller (Northern) Sea Lion

California Sea Lion

Tom Mangelsen

SIZE: Avg adult male 8 ft (2.4 m), 800 lbs. Avg adult female 5 ft (1.5 m), 250 lbs. At birth: 2.6 ft (0.8 m), 13 lbs.

BODY: Sleek body with elongate neck, **tapered snout,** and obvious ear pinnae. Adult males have **prominent sagittal crest** (raised forehead).

COLOR: Medium to **dark brown** when dry, **black when wet.**

BEHAVIOR: Gregarious. Often playful and trained for oceanarium shows. Vocalizations are **dog-like bark,** growl. Fast swimmers (15-20 mph). May dive to 450 ft (137 m) and stay down 20 min but shorter, shallower dives more common. Porpoising common.

HABITAT: Coastal. Remote, sandy island beaches used for rookeries. Haul out on shore, buoys, docks, rafts, etc.

FOOD HABITS: Opportunistic. Eat schooling fish, squid, rockfish, flatfish, hake, salmon, lamprey, dogfish.

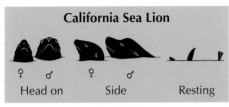

California Sea Lion

♀ ♂	♀ ♂	
Head on	Side	Resting

CAN BE CONFUSED WITH:

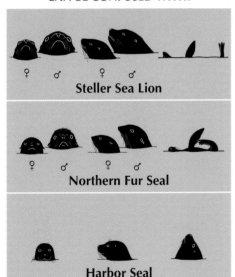

♀ ♂ ♀ ♂

Steller Sea Lion

♀ ♂ ♀ ♂

Northern Fur Seal

Harbor Seal

Distribution/Migration: Adult females remain near CA rookeries year-round. Some males move n. in summer-fall after breeding season. Sightings in AK waters are rare but increasing.

© 1990 Frank S. Balthis

Note differences in forehead profile and eye shape and angle of male California sea lion (L) and female Steller sea lion (R).

LIFE HISTORY: Sexually mature at 6-9 yrs. Single pup per yr born on rookeries in May-Jun after 11.5-mo gestation. Lactation lasts 12 mos. Dominant males hold territories about 30 days and breed polygynously with females within 2-3 wks of pupping. May live 15+ yrs.

STATUS AND HUMAN INTERACTIONS: Increasing. Minimum estimate CA to WA is 67,000. Numbers recovering after heavy exploitation in 1800s for meat and oil. Incidentally killed in net fisheries. Increasing conflicts with commercial and sport fisheries.

California Sea Lion

Zalophus californianus
Family: Otariidae

Steve McCutcheon

SIZE: Avg adult male 6.5 ft (2 m), 300-600 lbs. Avg adult female 4.2 ft (1.3 m), 65-110 lbs. At birth 2 ft. (0.6m), 11-12 lbs.

BODY: Small eared seal with **thick fur** and disproportionately **long hind flippers. Ears** tightly rolled and appear to be **located low on neck** (lower than eye level). **Head** round with **large eyes** and **short, conical snout.** Adult males have thickened neck and pronounced **furred crown.**

COLOR: Silver-gray to brown with lighter throat, appear black when wet. **Whiskers** black at birth and lighten with age until white by age 6-8 yrs.

BEHAVIOR: Inquisitive and mostly solitary at sea. Adults come ashore only briefly, congregate on rookeries annually to pup and breed. Dive up to 7 min to over 600 ft (180 m). Sleep with nose, one front, and both hind flippers above water ("jughandle" position) while at sea. Porpoising common.

Northern Fur Seal

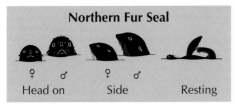

♀ ♂   ♀ ♂
Head on   Side   Resting

CAN BE CONFUSED WITH:

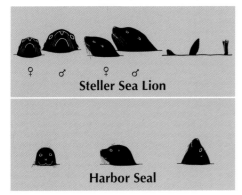

♀ ♂   ♀ ♂
Steller Sea Lion

Harbor Seal

Note dramatic differences in body size and shape, and coat of adult male (top) and female fur seal. ▶

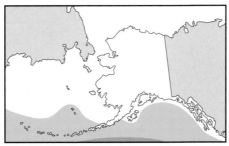

Distribution/Migration: N. Pacific. Long-distance seasonal migrants. Leave AK rookeries in Oct-Nov and remain offshore until Mar-Jun. Adult males overwinter in N. Pacific, females and subadult males spend winter offshore from SE Alaska to CA.

Tim Thompson

HABITAT: Primarily pelagic (7-10 mos per yr). Use remote islands as rookeries (primarily Pribilofs, but also San Miguel Is., CA).

FOOD HABITS: Feed primarily at night on variety of schooling fish and squid to 10 in. Herring, capelin, pollock, and squid important in AK waters.

LIFE HISTORY: Sexually mature at 4-5 yrs. Females breed late Jun-Jul with dominant males that establish and defend territories. Single pups born late Jun-Jul after gestation of 11.8 mos. Lactation lasts 4 mos; pups suckle intermittently between females' foraging trips at sea (up to 250 mi from rookery).

STATUS AND HUMAN INTERACTIONS: Depleted. Approx 1 million in e. Pacific and stable. Regulated commercial harvest on Pribilofs 1911-1984. Current annual subsistence harvest <2000 animals.

Northern Fur Seal

Callorhinus ursinus
Family: Otariidae

© 1990 Frank S. Balthis

SIZE: Avg adult male 14 ft (4.3 m), 2 tons. Avg adult female 10 ft (3 m), 1800 lbs. At birth 3.5 ft (1 m), 65 lbs.

BODY: Largest pinniped in N. Hemisphere. In males, **snout elongate, pendulous,** elephant-like. Broad, **earless,** round head. Nose of females and juveniles **extends slightly beyond mouth.**

COLOR: Pups born black, molt to silver at one mo. Adults are light brown.

BEHAVIOR: Polygynous breeders with social dominance hierarchy. Prevent overheating by flipping wet sand over back with front flippers. Make variety of multipitched cries, snorts, and grunts. Most remain at sea Apr-Dec. May spend 80-90% of this time diving. Deep, long divers with brief surface intervals. Usually dive <20 min to 1500 ft but are known to dive >3000 ft for up to 60 min.

HABITAT: Pelagic when at sea. Sandy CA beaches used for pupping, breeding, molting.

Northern Elephant Seal

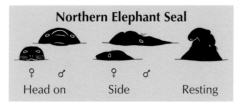

♀   ♂   ♀   ♂

Head on   Side   Resting

CAN BE CONFUSED WITH:

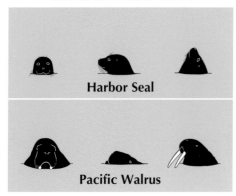

Harbor Seal

Pacific Walrus

Prominent nose extends past mouth even on elephant seal female (L) and juvenile male. ▶

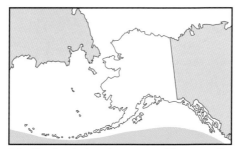

Distribution/Migration: N. Pacific. Long-distance seasonal migrant. Those in AK waters in Apr-Nov are mostly juveniles or adult males. Females remain off WA-OR coast.

Harriet Huber

FOOD HABITS: Fast while on land. At sea, feed on deepwater invertebrates and fish: whiting, ratfish, dogfish, rockfish, squid, octopus.

LIFE HISTORY: Sexually mature at 2-5 yrs. Adults arrive on rookeries Dec-Feb, single pup per yr born in Jan after gestation of 11 mos. Females fast during 28-day lactation and breed before pups are weaned. All return to sea by Feb-Mar. Remain at sea rest of year except during month-long molt (females in Apr-May, males in Jul-Aug).

STATUS AND HUMAN INTERACTIONS: Increasing throughout range. Approx 120,000 in N. Pacific. Commercial harvest in 1800s (for blubber) left only about 100 elephant seals at century's end. Protection has led to steady population increase. Occasionally caught incidentally in offshore fisheries from OR to Aleutians. Increasing frequency of AK sightings and strandings.

Northern Elephant Seal

Mirounga angustirostris
Family: Phocidae

Kathy Frost

SIZE: Avg adult male 7 ft (2.1m), 500 lbs. Avg adult female 7.5 ft (2.3 m), 500 lbs. At birth 4 ft (1.2 m), 75 lbs.

BODY: Largest ice-associated seal, relatively **small head, long whiskers,** and **square front flippers.**

COLOR: Tan to dark gray, often with reddish head and neck. Solid with no distinctive pattern or spots. **Pups** born silver-gray with distinctive **dark T-pattern** on face.

BEHAVIOR: Usually solitary except mother-pup pairs. Never far from edge of ice floe, with head toward water for escape. Swim at surface with **head and back above water.** Dive for up to 20 min to unknown depths.

HABITAT: Year-round association with moving ice. Usually avoid shorefast and thick, unbroken drift ice. Pups sometimes seen in rivers or open ocean.

FOOD HABITS: Benthic feeders. Eat primarily invertebrates (crabs, shrimp, clams, snails), saffron and arctic cod.

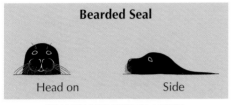

Bearded Seal

Head on   Side

CAN BE CONFUSED WITH:

Spotted Seal

Ribbon Seal

Ringed Seal

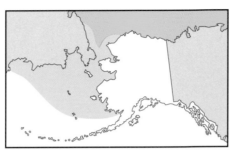

Distribution/Migration: Arctic-subarctic. Winter-spring in drifting ice of Bering and Chukchi seas. Move n. Apr-Jun with receding ice. Summer in Chukchi, Beaufort seas.

LIFE HISTORY: Sexually mature 5-7 yrs. Breed in May. Single pup per yr born on ice in Apr after 11-mo gestation. Lactation lasts only 12-18 days (pups triple in weight!). Annual molt May-Jun. May live 30 yrs.

STATUS AND HUMAN INTERACTIONS: Status unknown. Subsistence use by AK Natives for meat, fur, oil. AK subsistence and Russian commercial harvests may take 2000-4000 per yr.

Kathy Frost

Note dark T-pattern on silver face, and exposed back of swimming bearded seal pup.

Bearded Seal

Erignathus barbatus
Family: Phocidae

55

Tom Mangelsen

SIZE: Avg adult 6 ft (1.8 m), 250 lbs. At birth 3 ft (1 m), 25 lbs.

BODY: Medium, torpedo-shaped body with relatively **large, round head** and short limbs.

COLOR: Variable from nearly white to nearly black with variable, contrasting colored spots, rings, or blotches. Pups born with spotted silver coat.

BEHAVIOR: Usually solitary in water but haul out in groups of few to thousands. Inquisitive but elusive. May porpoise when swimming fast at the water surface. Dive <25 min, usually 5-8 min at depths to 600 ft (180 m).

HABITAT: Near-coastal, estuarine. May be seen miles up rivers. Haul out on remote intertidal sandbars, rocky shores, ice.

FOOD HABITS: Opportunistic. Eat wide variety of schooling fish, flatfish, crustaceans, squid.

Harbor Seal

Head on   Side   Resting

CAN BE CONFUSED WITH:

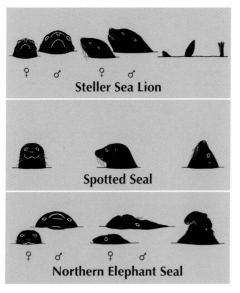

♀   ♂   ♀   ♂

Steller Sea Lion

Spotted Seal

♀   ♂   ♀   ♂

Northern Elephant Seal

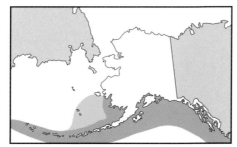

Distribution/Migration: N. Hemisphere. In e. N. Pacific, from s. CA to Pribilofs. Not migratory but make local seasonal movements in response to prey distribution.

© 1990 Frank S. Balthis

LIFE HISTORY: Sexually mature at 3-5 yrs. Breed Jul-Aug (in AK). Single pup per year, most born June (in AK) after 10-mo gestation. Pups weaned at 4-6 wks. Annual molt Aug-Sep in AK. Captive seals have lived 30+ yrs.

STATUS AND HUMAN INTERACTIONS: Healthy throughout range but declining in some AK areas. Estimated 70,000-75,000 in AK. Subsistence harvest by AK Natives of approx 2700/yr for meat, blubber, and hide. Serious localized fishery conflicts where seals steal fish from nets or are incidentally entangled. Are known to accumulate pollutants.

◄ **Note variable color pattern on harbor seal adults and pup.**

Harbor Seal

Phoca vitulina
Family: Phocidae

Kathy Frost

SIZE: Avg adult 5 ft (1.5 m), 150 lbs. At birth 3 ft (1 m), 25 lbs.

BODY: Medium size seal with long neck, large dark eyes. Fur has distinctive **color pattern.**

COLOR: All >1 yr old have **light bands on dark background** encircling the neck, each front flipper, and torso. Background darker on males than females. Pups born with lanugo, molt after 4 weeks to first-year coat of blue-gray back with light sides.

BEHAVIOR: Not wary when hauled out on ice. Run across ice (using alternating front legs, swinging hindquarters) rather than using caterpillar movement like most seals. **Seldom seen in water.** Surface with very little of head showing.

HABITAT: Ice-associated, rarely haul out on land. Southern edge of sea ice winter and spring. Probably pelagic summer and fall.

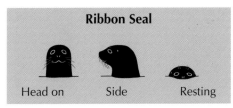

Ribbon Seal

| Head on | Side | Resting |

CAN BE CONFUSED WITH:

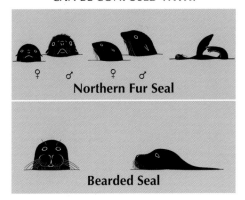

♀ ♂ ♀ ♂

Northern Fur Seal

Bearded Seal

Note low-contrast ribbon pattern on female and white coat of pup. ▶

Distribution/Migration: Arctic, N. Pacific. Follow ice: range farther s. in heavy ice (cold) years. Movements in ice-free months uncertain but probably pelagic in Bering and Chukchi seas.

Kathy Frost

FOOD HABITS: Eat a variety of pelagic fish and invertebrates: shrimp, crabs, squid, cod, sculpin, pollock, capelin, eelpouts.

LIFE HISTORY: Sexually mature at 3-5 yrs. Breed in May. Single pup per yr born early Apr on open ice floes after 11-mo gestation. Lactation is 3-4 wks. Molt annually before ice recedes (Mar-Jul). May live 30 yrs.

STATUS AND HUMAN INTERACTIONS: Status unknown. Heavy commercial harvest in 1960s by Soviet sealers has been reduced to about 4000 per yr. AK Native subsistence harvest of <100 per yr for meat, fur, oil.

Ribbon Seal

Phoca fasciata
Family: Phocidae

59

Lloyd Lowry

SIZE: Avg adult 5 ft (1.5 m), 210 lbs. At birth 3 ft (1 m), 26 lbs.

BODY: Medium-size seal with **narrow, dog-like snou**t.

COLOR: Dark irregular spots scattered on silver sides and darker back. Pups born with lanugo, molt to adult coat in 3-4 weeks.

BEHAVIOR: Haul out on ice floes late fall to early summer and on land during warmer mos. Often form triads of female, male, and pup during pupping and breeding season. Gregarious at other times. Known to dive to bottom in waters >800 ft (245 m) deep.

HABITAT: Continental shelf to coastal. **Seasonally associated with ice front.** Avoid heavy ice but use floes at ice front fall to summer. In summer, found near shore, on land, and up rivers as well as far offshore.

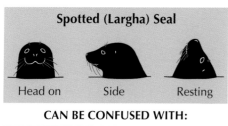

Spotted (Largha) Seal

| Head on | Side | Resting |

CAN BE CONFUSED WITH:

Harbor Seal

Ringed Seal

Ribbon Seal

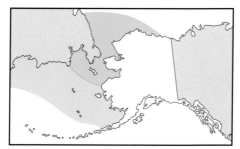

Distribution/Migration: Arctic, N. Pacific. In Bering Sea ice front late fall to spring. As ice recedes, move n. and toward coast. Migrate offshore when fast ice forms on shore.

Kathy Frost

Note female's dog-like snout and black-spotted light coat. Pup has white coat.

FOOD HABITS: Opportunistic. Eat small schooling fish, shrimp, octopus.

LIFE HISTORY: Sexually mature at 3-5 yrs. Breed Apr-May. Single pup per yr born on ice in Apr after 11-mo gestation. Females use shelter of ice hummocks rather than digging lair. Pups wean after 3-4 wks. Annual molt May-Jun. May live 35 yrs.

STATUS AND HUMAN INTERACTIONS: Status unknown. Limited commercial harvest by Russia. Subsistence use by AK and Siberian Natives is approx 3000 per yr. Potential competition with commercial fisheries (shrimp, pollock, herring).

Brendan Kelly

SIZE: Avg adults 4 ft (1.2 m), 120 lbs. At birth 2 ft (0.6 m), 9 lbs.

BODY: Smallest ice-associated seal. **Shor**t and **round** body. Well-developed **claws** on front flippers. **Short snout** makes face cat-like.

COLOR: Gray background with **light rings around black spots** on back and sides. Breeding males have a **dark face.** Pups born with lanugo, molt after 4-6 weeks to dark gray back and silver sides.

BEHAVIOR: Use claws to maintain breathing holes and dig lairs on stable fast ice. Generally docile but wary while hauled out on ice. Haul out in center of ice floes with head toward hole. Spend most of nonbreeding months feeding in water near or under pack ice. Surface briefly between dives 1-7 min long to 200 ft or less. Known to dive >600 ft (180 m).

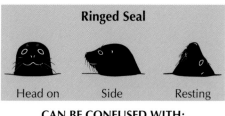

Ringed Seal

Head on   Side   Resting

CAN BE CONFUSED WITH:

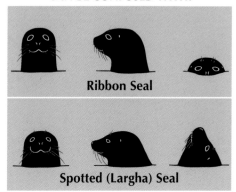

Ribbon Seal

Spotted (Largha) Seal

Note ringed seal's short snout, well-developed claws, and proximity to water-access hole. ▶

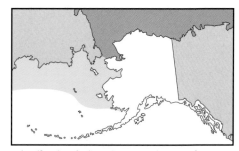

Distribution/Migration: Arctic. Northern-most distribution for AK seal: from Bristol Bay n. into Chukchi and Beaufort seas. Associated with ice year-round. In summer, move n. with receding permanent ice.

Lori Quakenbush

HABITAT: Year-round association with ice. Adults spend breeding season on stable landfast ice, nonbreeders in moving pack ice. Juveniles may be found in open water.

FOOD HABITS: Eat variety of small crustaceans, zooplankton, schooling fish.

LIFE HISTORY: Sexually mature at 5-7 yrs. Breed Apr-May. Single pup per yr born in Apr after 11-mo gestation. Pups usually born in lair excavated in snow on shorefast ice, and wean after 5-7 wks on diet of 45-50% milk fat. Peak of molt in Jun. Seals haul out on ice at holes or edge of leads to bask in sun. May live 40 yrs.

STATUS AND HUMAN INTERACTIONS: Assumed stable. Approx one million in Bering, Chukchi, and Beaufort seas; 6-7 million worldwide. No commercial harvest. Subsistence use by AK Natives is approx 5000 per yr for fur, meat, oil.

Ringed Seal

Phoca hispida
Family: Phocidae

Kathy Frost

SIZE: Avg adult male 10 ft (3 m), 1.3 tons. Avg adult female 8.5 ft (2.6 m), 1 ton. At birth 4 ft (1.2 m), 150 lbs.

BODY: Robust body covered with short coarse fur. Relatively **small head** with wide, whiskered snout. Both sexes have **tusks** extending down from corners of mouth. No pinnae present.

COLOR: Pink to cinnamon-brown. Almost white after immersion in cold water. Calves born dark gray-brown.

BEHAVIOR: Gregarious, form tight piles on haulouts. Quadrupedal locomotion on land. Use tusks for hauling out on ice, pup defense, and aggression but not for digging. Sexes segregated except during breeding season. Shallow divers, usually 6-10 min to 30-150 ft (9-46 m).

HABITAT: Continental shelf and coastal. Use moving pack ice for resting, pupping, molting. Also haul out on secluded rocky shores or islands if no ice available.

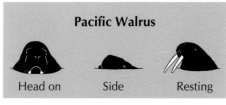

Pacific Walrus

Head on — Side — Resting

CAN BE CONFUSED WITH:

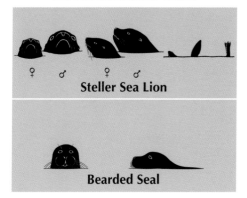

♀   ♂   ♀   ♂

Steller Sea Lion

Bearded Seal

Note square snout and round head profiles (females and calf). ▶

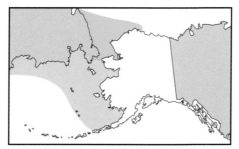

Distribution/Migration: Arctic and N. Pacific. Winter in Bering Sea pack ice. Follow receding ice n., summer at ice edge in Chukchi Sea, and move s. in advance of ice edge. Some males summer in Bristol Bay. Also seen in Cook Inlet.

Kathy Frost

FOOD HABITS: Benthic feeders. Eat primarily mollusks and other invertebrates but also fish and other marine mammals. Appear to use whiskers to find bivalves and suction to remove meat from the shells.

LIFE HISTORY: Sexually mature at 6-10 yrs. Breed polygynously Jan-Mar. Single calf every 2+ yrs born on ice Apr-May after gestation of 15 mos. Weaned at 2 yrs. Male calves stay with mother 2-5 yrs, female calves stay with female herd. Annual molt Jun-Aug. May live 30 yrs.

STATUS AND HUMAN INTERACTIONS: Stable or slow decrease. Approx 240,000 in Bering and Chukchi seas. Severely depleted by commercial harvests from 1600s to 1950s. Pacific population recovered after this harvest ended. Subsistence use by AK Natives and commercial Russian harvest averaged 8000-12,000 per yr in 1980s.

Pacific Walrus

Odobenus rosmarus
Family: Odobenidae

Two Alaska marine mammals are included in this guide that are neither pinniped nor cetacean: the polar bear and sea otter. They are both fissipeds, "split-footed" members of the order Carnivora, and are more closely related to terrestrial carnivores, like weasels, than seals or whales. Evolutionary newcomers to the marine environment, these species lack many of the physiologic adaptations to marine life seen in pinnipeds and cetaceans. Both species are considered marine mammals under U.S. laws because of the roles they play in the marine environment.

Polar bears, in the bear family (Ursidae), spend most of their lives associated with marine ice and waters. Although competent swimmers, they are the marine mammal least adapted to aquatic existence. They rest, mate, give birth, and suckle their young on the ice.

Sea otters, in the weasel family (Mustelidae), live a primarily marine life: they rest, mate, give birth, and suckle their young in the water. Their hind limbs are webbed for swimming, but their front paws are padded with separate, clawed digits. They lack blubber, but are insulated by air trapped in their thick fur, which is densest among all mammals.

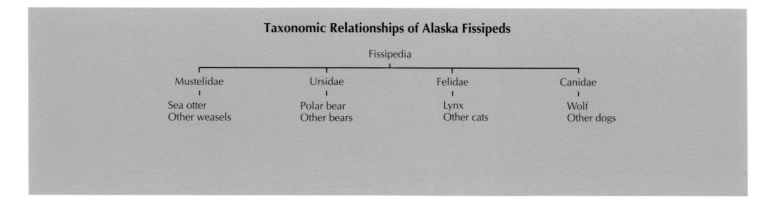

Taxonomic Relationships of Alaska Fissipeds

Fissipedia

Mustelidae	Ursidae	Felidae	Canidae
Sea otter	Polar bear	Lynx	Wolf
Other weasels	Other bears	Other cats	Other dogs

Some terrestrial (land-based) mammals can be confused with marine mammals when seen swimming in coastal marine waters. Although their silhouette head profiles may be similar, the swimming behavior of terrestrial and marine mammals differs and may be used to distinguish the two groups.

Most terrestrial mammals like bears, deer, and moose rarely submerge, and their backs may be visible while they are swimming. Beavers, mink, and river otters may submerge momentarily but resurface within seconds. Although river otters swim and roll at the surface like sea otters, they never float on their backs. Continued observation of a swimming mammal's behavior may be required to distinguish terrestrial from marine species.

Rarely Submerge

Deer   Bear

Moose

May Submerge Briefly

River Otter   Beaver

Other Mammals

Tom Mangelsen

SIZE: Avg adult male 8.5 ft (2.6 m), 900 lbs. Avg adult female 6.5 ft (2 m), 500 lbs. At birth: 10 in (0.3 m), 1-2 lbs.

BODY: Large, **long-legged** bear with dense fur and blubber layer. Prominent snout and **short, round, furred ears.**

COLOR: White with black eyes, nose, and lips.

BEHAVIOR: Usually solitary except female-cub groups or near abundant food source. Pregnant females den up for winter but do not hibernate. All age and sex classes may den temporarily to avoid harsh weather. Very inquisitive, with an acute sense of smell. Swim with head above water, dog-paddling with front legs. Dive to approach basking seals at edge of floes or to flee from humans.

HABITAT: Spend entire life associated with pack ice. Females may prefer shorefast ice while others prefer moving sea ice at the floe edge. Usually within 180 mi of shore.

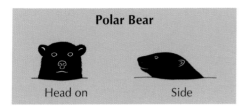

Polar Bear

Head on   Side

Distribution/Migration: Arctic. From Bering Sea into Chukchi and Beaufort seas. Seasonal movement with ice: n. in summer as ice recedes from coast, s. with advancing ice in fall.

Steve McCutcheon

Polar bears rest, mate, give birth, and suckle their young on the ice.

Polar bears dog-paddle with head and much of back above water. ▶

Kathy Frost

FOOD HABITS: Eat primarily ringed and bearded seals. Catch seals mainly by still-hunting at breathing holes, haul-outs, and lairs, or stalking basking seals. Occasionally eat other mammals, eggs, vegetation, beach-cast carrion.

LIFE HISTORY: Sexually mature at 4-8 yrs. Breed polygamously Apr-Jun. 1-3 cubs every 28 mos. Pregnant females dig a den Oct-Dec where cubs are born Dec-Jan and stay until Mar-Apr. Lactation lasts 28 mos. May live to 25-30 yrs.

STATUS AND HUMAN INTERACTION: Population healthy and apparently increased 1960-70s. Approx 3000-5000 in AK (1986 estimate). Sport hunters killed approx 200 per yr from 1940s until banned in 1972. Subsistence use (for hide, meat, handicraft) by AK Natives since 1980 was approx 130 per yr.

Polar Bear

Ursus maritimus
Family: Ursidae

Kate Wynne

SIZE: Avg adult male 5 ft (1.5 m), 70 lbs. Avg adult female 4 ft (1.2 m), 60 lbs. At birth 10 in (0.3 m), 5 lbs.

BODY: Largest member of the weasel family, smallest marine mammal. **Long, flat tail** and webbed hind feet. Retractable claws on front paws. Head round with **small eyes, triangular nose, and visible ear pinnae.** Densest fur of any mammal (no blubber).

COLOR: Body dark brown to blond with lighter head. Head and neck lighten with age until **white** in **old** animals.

BEHAVIOR: Usually swim on back with feet in the air but may swim on stomach, porpoise, and roll repeatedly while traveling. Groom fur frequently. Eat only while floating. Groom, rest, and nurse young while floating or hauled out on rocky shores or sandbars. Front paws used for foraging and grooming but not swimming. Form sex-segregated groups. Hundreds may float together in "raft"

Sea Otter

| Head on | Side | Resting |

CAN BE CONFUSED WITH:

River Otter

♀ ♂ ♀ ♂

Northern Fur Seal

Note small eyes, large nose, and head angle of an inquisitive otter (R) and typical resting posture of a blond-headed adult. ▶

Distribution/Migration: N. Pacific. AK population ranges from Aleutians to Prince William Sound and SE AK. Non-migratory but move in response to prey abundance.

Kennan Ward

while resting. Short and shallow divers, usually <100 ft for 1-2 min.

HABITAT: Coastal. Shallow waters with rocky or sandy substrate.

FOOD HABITS: Eat primarily benthic invertebrates: clams, mussels, urchins, crabs, fish. Capable of dramatically affecting size and abundance of prey.

LIFE HISTORY: Sexually mature at 3-6 yrs. Peak breeding Sep-Oct in AK. Single pup per 1+ yrs after variable gestation of 5-8 mos. In AK, most pups born in May (on land or water) and are dependent on mother for 5-12 mos.

STATUS AND HUMAN INTERACTIONS: Numbers increasing. Approx 150,000 in AK waters. Nearly extinct because of heavy commercial harvests until protected in 1911. Most of historic range in AK repopulated. Subsistence and handicraft use of pelts by AK Natives. Known to compete with shellfisheries and to entangle in coastal gillnets.

Sea Otter

Enhydra lutris
Family: Mustelidae

The following terms are defined as they are used in this book.

Amphibious: Lives both on land and in water.

Amphipod: Small crustacean with laterally compressed body, in the order Amphipoda.

Baleen: Bony material formed into comb-like plates, grows from upper jaw of mysticete whales.

Benthic: Associated with the ocean bottom.

Blow: Moist air forcefully exhaled from lungs and through the blowhole of a surfacing cetacean.

Bowride: Swim in the wake created by a moving boat, often at the bow or front of the boat.

Breach: Jump clear of the water surface.

Carnivore: Flesh eater, member of the taxonomic order Carnivora.

Cetacean: Whale, dolphin, or porpoise; member of the order Cetacea.

Chevron: V-shaped stripes.

Coastal: Waters adjacent to coastline.

Copepod: Small crustacean in the class Copepoda.

Depleted Status: Species whose numbers are below its optimal sustainable population level.

Dimorphism: Two different forms or traits. Sexual dimorphism: traits differ between sexes.

Dive pattern: Typical pattern and timing of a whale's blows and dives.

Echolocation: Means of locating prey and other objects by generating and receiving sound signals (sonar).

Endangered Status: Species in danger of extinction in all or a significant portion of its range.

Euphausid: Small shrimp-like crustacean in the order Euphausiacea. Also called krill.

Falcate: Strongly curved or hooked.

Fissiped: "Split-footed" carnivores, including weasels, bears, cats, dogs, and raccoons; members of the suborder Fissipedia, order Carnivora.

Fluke: Flat propelling surface of cetacean tail (see p. 6).

Gestation: Carrying young in the uterus until delivery.

Haul out (verb): To rest onshore.

Haulout (noun): Shoreside resting site.

Lactation: Production of milk by female; duration of suckling.

Lair: Den

Lanugo: Long white fur retained by some seal pups after birth.

Lobtail: Slap water surface with tail.

Melon: Bulbous forehead of toothed

whales; contains nasal passages and fat (see p. 6).

Molt: Shedding and replacing fur.

Monogamous: One male mates with one female.

Morphology: Body form, shape or structure.

Opportunist: Eats a variety of prey, usually what is most easily accessible.

Pack Ice: Mass of broken ice pieces, at edge of permanent sea ice.

Pelagic: Associated with deep, open water.

Pinna: External ear flap (plural: pinnae).

Pinniped: "Fin-footed" carnivores, including seals, sea lions, and walrus: members of the suborder Pinnipedia, order Carnivora.

Piscivore: Fish eater.

Pod: Group of cetaceans traveling together.

Polygynous: One male mates with more than one female.

Porpoising: Non-cetacean behavior of breaking water surface while swimming fast.

Quadrupedal: Four-legged mobility.

Rookery: Haulout used by pinnipeds for pupping and breeding.

Rostrum: Upper jaw (see p. 6).

Sexual maturity: Age at which animal is first capable of breeding.

Spatulate: Broad, flat, round shape.

Specialist: Eats a limited number of prey species.

Spyhop: Poke head vertically out of the water.

Taxonomy: Classification of organisms according to how they are related to one another.

Threatened Status: Species likely to become endangered within foreseeable future in all or significant portion of its range.

Zooplankton: Minute animals adrift in water column, including early life stages of fish and invertebrates. Includes copepods and amphipods.

Abbreviations

approx	approximately
avg	average
e.	east or eastern
ft	foot or feet
hr	hour
in.	inches
lb	pound
m	meter
max	maximum
min	minute
mo	month
mph	miles per hour
n.	north or northern
s.	south or southern
sec	seconds
w.	west or western
wt	weight
yr	year
♀	female
♂	male
<	less than
>	greater than

PAGE	English (common)	Latin (scientific)	Japanese	Russian	Alaska Native
CETACEANS					
Mysticetes					
8	Bowhead whale	*Balaena mysticetus*	hokkyoku kujira	grendlandskiy	agyaax̂[1], agviq[3]
10	Northern right whale	*Eubalaena glacialis*	semi kujira	yuzhnyy kit	kulumax̂[1]
12	Blue whale	*Balaenoptera musculus*	shiro nagasu kujira		umĝulix̂[1]
14	Fin whale	*B. physalus*	nagasu kujira	finval	mangidax̂[1]
16	Sei whale	*B. borealis*	iwashi kujira	seyval	alamax̂chx̂ix̂[1]
18	Minke whale	*B. acutorostrata*	koiwashi kujira	zalivov, minke	agamaxchix̂[1]
20	Humpback whale	*Megaptera novaeangliae*	zato kujira	gorbach	alamax̂[1]
22	Gray whale	*Eschrichtius robustus*	koku kujira	seryy kit	chickakhluk[6]
Odontocetes					
24	Sperm whale	*Physeter macrocephalus*	makko kujira	kashalot	agdax̂xix̂[1]
26	Belukha whale	*Delphinapterus leucas*	shiro iruka	belukha	alam quhmaa[1], sisuaq[3]
28	Baird's beaked (bottlenose) whale	*Berardius bairdii*	tsuchi kujira	severnyy plavun	chiidux̂[1]
30	Cuvier's beaked (goosebeak) whale	*Ziphius cavirostris*	akabo kujira	kyuv'erov	chumchugagakh[6]
32	Stejneger's (Bering Sea) beaked whale	*Mesoplodon stejnegeri*	ogiha kujira	remnezub Stegnegera	kigan agaliusiak[6]
34	Killer whale (orca)	*Orcinus orca*	shachi	kosatka	aglux̂[1]
36	Pacific white-sided dolphin	*Lagenorhynchus obliquidens*	kama iruka	belobokii delfin	
38	Dall's porpoise	*Phocoenoides dalli*	rikuzen iruka	belokrylka	kdangix̂[1]
40	Harbor porpoise	*Phocoena phocoena*	nezumi iruka	morskaja svinya	alaadax̂[1]

PAGE	English (common)	Latin (scientific)	Japanese	Russian	Alaska Native
PINNIPEDS					
Otariids					
46	Steller (northern) sea lion	_Eumetopias jubatus_	todo	sivuch	qawax̂[1], uginaq[2], taan[4], wiinaq[5]
48	California sea lion	_Zalophus californianus_	kariforunia ashika	morskoi lev	
50	Northern fur seal	_Callorhinus ursinus_	kita ottosei	severhyi morski kotik	hlaaqudas[1], aataak[2]
Phocids					
52	Northern elephant seal	_Mirounga angustirostris_	kita zou azarashi	morski slon	
54	Bearded seal	_Erignathus barbatus_	agohige-azarashi	morski zayatz (lakhtak)	mukluk[2], ugruk[3]
56	Harbor seal	_Phoca vitulina_	gomafu-azarashi	obykhovennyi tyulen	isuĝix̂[1], tsaa[4], tsuwiq[5]
58	Ribbon seal	_P. fasciata_	kurakake-azarashi	polosatyi tyulen (krylatka)	qasruliq[2], quigulik[3]
60	Spotted (largha) seal	_P. largha_	komimi-azarashi	larga	ukutux̂[1], issuriq[2], qasigiaq[3]
62	Ringed seal	_P. hispida_	fuiri-azarashi	kolchataya nerpa (akiba)	nayiq[2], natchiq[3]
Odobenid					
64	Pacific walrus	_Odobenus rosmarus_	seiuchi	morzh	amgaadax̂[1], asveq[2], aiviq[3]
MARINE FISSIPEDS					
68	Polar bear	_Ursus maritimus_	shiro kuma	belyi medved	kdam tanĝaaĝa[1], arlunaq[2], nanuq[3]
70	Sea otter	_Enhydra lutris_	rakko	morskaya vydra	chngatux̂[1], aarnaq[2], yùxwch´[4]

Alaska Native: 1 = Unangax̂ (western Aleutians and Pribilof Aleut),   2 = Yupik,   3 = Inupiat,   4 = Tlingit,   5 = Alutiiq,   6 = Aleut